A Closer Look at
LIVING THINGS

A Closer Look at
LIVING THINGS

Edited by Michael Anderson

Britannica®
Educational Publishing
IN ASSOCIATION WITH

ROSEN
EDUCATIONAL SERVICES

Published in 2012 by Britannica Educational Publishing
(a trademark of Encyclopædia Britannica, Inc.)
in association with Rosen Educational Services, LLC
29 East 21st Street, New York, NY 10010.

Distributed exclusively by Rosen Educational Services.
For a listing of additional Britannica Educational Publishing titles, call toll free (800) 237-9932.

First Edition

Britannica Educational Publishing
Michael I. Levy: Executive Editor, Encyclopædia Britannica
J.E. Luebering: Director, Core Reference Group, Encyclopædia Britannica
Adam Augustyn: Assistant Manager, Encyclopædia Britannica

Anthony L. Green: Editor, Compton's by Britannica
Michael Anderson: Senior Editor, Compton's by Britannica
Sherman Hollar: Associate Editor, Compton's by Britannica

Marilyn L. Barton: Senior Coordinator, Production Control
Steven Bosco: Director, Editorial Technologies
Lisa S. Braucher: Senior Producer and Data Editor
Yvette Charboneau: Senior Copy Editor
Kathy Nakamura: Manager, Media Acquisition

Rosen Educational Services
Jeanne Nagle: Senior Editor
Nelson Sá: Art Director
Cindy Reiman: Photography Manager
Karen Huang: Photo Researcher
Matthew Cauli: Designer, Cover Design
Introduction by Jeanne Nagle

Library of Congress Cataloging-in-Publication Data

A closer look at living things / edited by Michael Anderson.
    p. cm.—(The Environment: Ours to Save)
"In association with Britannica Educational Publishing, Rosen Educational Services."
Includes bibliographical references and index.
ISBN 978-1-61530-533-9 (library binding)
1. Organisms—Juvenile literature. 2. Life (Biology)—Juvenile literature. I. Anderson, Michael, 1972-
QH309.2.C564 2012
578—dc22

2011011720

Manufactured in the United States of America

On the cover: A hippopotamus, a huge mammal that lives in eastern Africa, is seen against the back-
drop of Ngorongoro Crater, a nature reserve in East Africa. *Shutterstock.com*

Interior background images Shutterstock.com

CONTENTS

The world is filled with living and nonliving things. In most cases, figuring out which of them are alive is easy. For instance, it's obvious that a fuzzy woodland creature scampering across a field is alive, while a rock plunked down in the middle of that same field is not. Science, however, doesn't leave such things to casual observation. In order for an organism to be alive, it must pass a series of seven tests.

One test concerns movement. Living things are able to get from one location to another, or they at least have movement within themselves. For an example of the second type of movement, consider a tree. It can't move from one place to another, but it does have the ability to move water, nutrients, and other materials internally. Whatever the type of motion, it must occur under the organism's own power. Being pushed, pulled, or otherwise forced to move doesn't count.

A second test is sensitivity. Living organisms respond to conditions in their environment using whatever senses they have. Plants stretch and grow toward sunlight. Animals and people flinch when they hear a loud sound or feel a sharp touch.

The ability to gather nutrients (the source of energy) from food sources is another test that proves something is alive. Eating other organisms is how most animals, including humans, obtain energy. Plants make their own food through a chemical process known as photosynthesis. Some food energy is used right away, while some is stored for later use.

The process used to create energy from food is another essential characteristic of living things. It's called respiration. In most cases, respiration involves the exchange of oxygen and carbon dioxide, a process that releases energy. Humans and land animals inhale oxygen and exhale carbon dioxide from the air using lungs. Fish and many other aquatic animals don't have lungs but are able to absorb oxygen and expel carbon dioxide through structures called gills. Plants absorb and push out gases through stomata, or pores, in their leaves.

Living things grow, meaning new cells are added on to or replace old cells that make up an organism's body. Examples of growth include legs or stems getting longer, teeth sprouting through the gums of youngsters, and new layers of skin or wood that cover and heal wounds. In a few special cases, plants

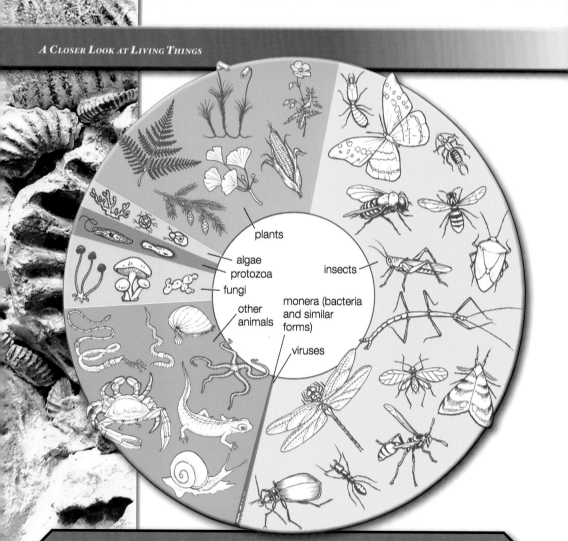

plants

algae
protozoa
fungi
other
animals

insects

monera (bacteria
and similar
forms)

viruses

Scientists have discovered nearly 2 million different species, or kinds, of living things. Most of these species are animals. About half of all species are the animals known as insects. **Encyclopædia Britannica, Inc.**

and animals can replace a body part that has been lost—a tail, for example—through a process called regeneration.

A living organism also has to be able to create more of its kind through reproduction.

Living things reproduce either sexually, with two parents, or asexually, where an organism creates new life on its own.

The final test that every living thing must pass is the ability to get rid of waste and toxic substances through excretion. These unwanted and potentially harmful materials are produced in plants, animals, and humans in the process of living. Plants release waste gases into the air through their stomata. Animals and humans sweep waste and toxins out of their bodies primarily through sweat, urine, and feces.

The ability to do just one or a few of the functions listed here is all well and good, but that doesn't mean that something is alive. All seven characteristics must be present for an organism to be considered a true living thing.

CHAPTER 1

THE CHARACTERISTICS OF LIVING THINGS

Living things include many kinds of organisms, from the plants, animals, fungi, and algae that can be readily seen in nature, to the multitude of tiny creatures known as protozoa, bacteria, and archaea that can be seen only with a microscope. Living things can be found in every type of habitat on Earth—on land and in lakes, rivers, and oceans. Although all these organisms are very different from one another, they all have two things in common: They are descended from a single ancient ancestor, and they are alive.

Most scientists believe that the first living organism on Earth probably evolved within a billion years of Earth's formation, which occurred roughly 4.5 billion years ago. This belief is based on evidence from the fossil record. Fossil remains of microorganisms resembling cyanobacteria (a group of microorganisms formerly known as blue-green algae) were discovered embedded in rocks that were roughly 3.5 billion years old.

The colors of Morning Glory Pool, a hot spring in Yellowstone National Park, are the result of different types of cyanobacteria, which are microorganisms that thrive in harsh environments. Shutterstock.com

The early Earth was very different from the Earth of today. The atmosphere was rich in hydrogen, which was critical to the chemical events that later took place. According to one scientific hypothesis, soupy mixtures of elements important to life, such as carbon,

nitrogen, oxygen, and hydrogen, were concentrated in warm pools bathed in the ultraviolet rays of the Sun. Out of this mix, chemical elements combined in reactions that grew increasingly complex, forming organic molecules such as proteins and nucleic acids. As they combined and recombined, these molecules eventually formed a highly primitive cell capable of reproducing itself. Over millions of years, the process of natural selection then aided the evolution of single- and multicelled organisms from an ancient common ancestor.

There are seven key functions, or processes, necessary for life. To be categorized as a living thing, an organism must be able to do all of these.

MOVEMENT

Living things have the ability to move in some way without outside help. The movement may consist of the flow of material within the organism or external movement of the organism or parts of the organism.

SENSITIVITY

Living things respond to conditions around them. For example, green plants grow toward sunshine, certain microorganisms shrink into tiny balls when something touches them, and human beings blink when light shines into their eyes.

RESPIRATION

All living organisms must be capable of releasing energy stored in food molecules through a chemical process known as cellular respiration. In aerobic respiration, oxygen is taken up and carbon dioxide is given off. In single-celled organisms, the exchange of these gases with the environment occurs across the organism's cellular membrane. In multicellular organisms, the exchange of the gases with the environment is slightly more complex and usually involves some type of organ specially adapted for this purpose. Large multicellular animals such as birds and mammals must breathe in oxygen, which travels to the lungs and is transferred to the blood flow of the body's arteries. The arterial system carries this fresh oxygen to all the tissues and cells of the body, where it is exchanged for carbon dioxide, a cellular waste product that must be carried back to the lungs so that the organism can exhale it.

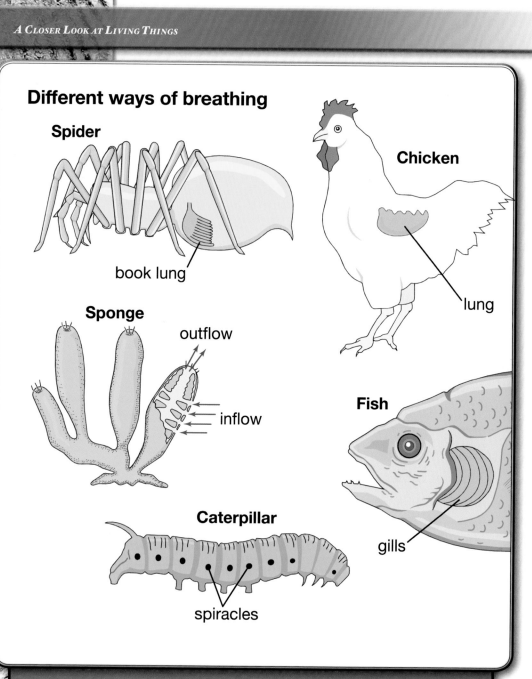

Different ways of breathing

Spider

book lung

Chicken

lung

Sponge

outflow

inflow

Fish

gills

Caterpillar

spiracles

Insects breathe through holes in the sides of their bodies. Fish and young amphibians have organs called gills to take in oxygen from water. Mammals, birds, reptiles, and adult amphibians breathe through lungs. **Encyclopædia Britannica, Inc.**

Plants respire too, but they do it through openings called stomata, which are found on the underside of their leaves. Certain types of bacteria and archaea use a type of cellular respiration, called anaerobic respiration, in which the role of oxygen is carried out by other substances. Anaerobic respiration may make use of carbon dioxide or nitrate, nitrite, or sulfate ions, and it allows the organism to live in an environment without oxygen.

NUTRITION

Living things require energy to survive. The energy is derived from nutrients, or food. Green plants, algae, and certain archaea and bacteria can make food from water and carbon dioxide via photosynthesis. Plants called legumes can make proteins by taking up nitrogen provided by bacteria that live in nodules in the plant's roots. Animals, fungi, protozoa, and many archaea and bacteria need to get food from an outside source. They do this in different ways, all of which depend on what physical adaptations the organism has. Some animals such as mammals bite into their food with teeth, while certain insects suck up nectar from flowers.

A bear gnaws on the bones of an animal it has killed and consumed.
© www.istockphoto.com/Len Tillim

Many species of protozoa and bacteria take in nutrients through membranes that cover their bodies.

Regardless of how the nutrients are obtained—or, in the case of autotrophic organisms, manufactured—the organism's physical state will determine how the nutrients are used. Some of the nutrients may be used for structural repairs—that is, turned into living material, such as bones, teeth, scales, or wood. Some portion of nutrients may be used to provide energy, which the organism needs in order to function. This can be compared to the process in which an engine burns oil or coal and gets energy to move a train. But note that an engine does not use coal or oil to make itself larger or mend parts, as living things do with food.

GROWTH

Snowballs will grow in size when they are rolled through snow and salt crystals will grow in salty water as it evaporates. Although these lifeless objects become larger, they do not grow in the way that living things do. Living things grow by making new parts and materials and changing old ones. This

Regeneration

The process by which plants and animals replace lost or damaged parts by growing them anew is called regeneration. Often the growth is abnormal in appearance but completely functional. A tree trunk that is burned will produce a new covering for the vital vascular strands that transport water and food, though the bark may be scarred. A deep cut on human skin will eventually close with new skin growth, leaving a scar.

Some animals possess the ability to completely regenerate a missing part. Lizards can regenerate a new tail, and salamanders can replace a limb or even an eye. In humans the liver can regenerate after partial destruction. To some extent plants form new meristem (growth) tissues and produce new shoots after the tops are pruned.

happens when a seed grows into a plant or a chick matures into a hen. As human beings grow, they add new structures, such as teeth, and change the proportions of others.

A special kind of growth heals injuries. Shrubs and trees mend injuries by covering them with bark and adding new layers of wood. Crabs grow new legs when old ones

are lost. Human beings can heal cut skin and mend broken bones.

REPRODUCTION

When living things reproduce, they make new living things. This is true even of the simplest microorganisms, which may reproduce by simply dividing into two parts. Each new part is able to move, feed, grow, and perform the other functions of living. This type of reproduction is called asexual, because it can be performed without a mating partner. There are other forms of

Some species of whiptail lizards are able to reproduce asexually. Females lay eggs that have not been fertilized by a male but still produce normal young. © www.istockphoto.com/ Nancy Nehring

asexual reproduction, in addition to sexual reproduction, which requires a partner.

Asexual reproduction is most commonly found among the so-called lower organisms, such as bacteria and some types of protozoa and fungi. They are called "lower" not because they are unimportant or simple, but rather because they evolved earlier than the complex "higher" organisms, such as vertebrates. Mammals and birds, for example, require a partner to reproduce. Some higher organisms, however, are able to reproduce asexually. Certain plants are an example of this, as are some reptiles.

EXCRETION

All living organisms create waste products via the processes of living. Much waste comes from food. The rest is produced by movement, growth, and other functions of living. If this waste remained in living things, it would soon cause illness and death. Thus living things must have a way to dispose of waste matter. The process that removes waste products from the body is called excretion.

CHAPTER 2

CELLS, TISSUES, AND ORGANS

C ells are the building blocks of the living world. Living things as diverse as bacteria, archaea, algae, fungi, protozoans, animals, and plants all consist of one or more cells, which are made up of components that help living organisms eat, respire, excrete wastes, and perform all of the necessary functions of life. The components are organized, which means that they fit and work together. For this reason, living things are called organisms. Similar cells that work together form structures called tissues, and groups of tissues form organs.

EUKARYOTES, PROKARYOTES, AND VIRUSES

The activities of the cells are controlled by the cell's genetic material—its DNA. In some types of organisms, called eukaryotes, the DNA is contained within a membrane-bound structure called the nucleus. The term eukaryote derives from the Greek *eu* (true) and *karyon* (nucleus.) In eukaryotic cells, most specialized tasks, such as obtaining

Animal cell

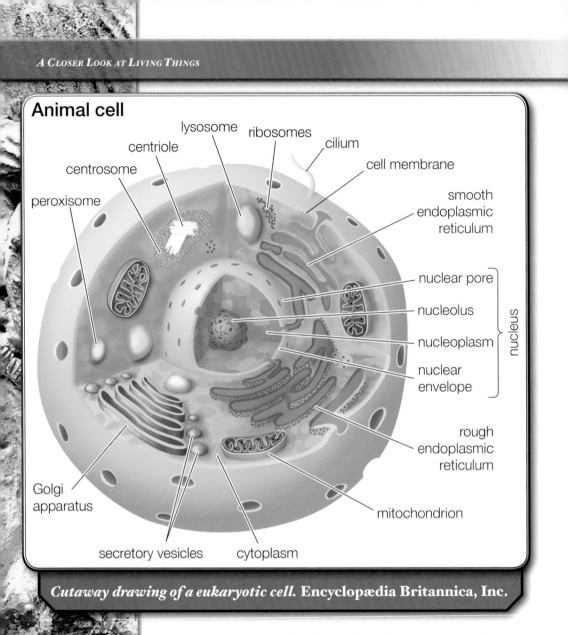

centrosome
peroxisome
centriole
lysosome
ribosomes
cilium
cell membrane
smooth endoplasmic reticulum
nuclear pore
nucleolus
nucleoplasm
nuclear envelope
nucleus
rough endoplasmic reticulum
mitochondrion
Golgi apparatus
secretory vesicles
cytoplasm

Cutaway drawing of a eukaryotic cell. **Encyclopædia Britannica, Inc.**

energy from food molecules and producing material for cell growth, occur within a number of enclosed bodies called organelles. Many microorganisms, namely bacteria and archaea, consist of a single cell lacking this

complex structure, and their DNA is not contained in a distinct nucleus. These organisms are called prokaryotes, from the Greek *pro* (before) and *karyon*.

Prokaryotic organisms are believed to have evolved before eukaryotes. Prokaryotic organisms such as the cyanobacteria can photosynthesize food; their food-making chlorophyll is scattered through the cell. In eukaryotic photosynthesizing organisms, such as plants and algae, the chlorophyll is contained within chloroplasts. Most bacteria have neither nuclei nor chloroplasts and are heterotrophic, meaning they must obtain their food from other organisms.

Scientists once believed that prokaryotic organisms were the simplest organisms. Then viruses were discovered. A virus is a very small infective particle composed of a nucleic acid core and a protein capsule. Viruses are responsible for many diseases of plants and animals, and some even infect bacteria and archaea. A virus is not a cell itself, but it requires a cell of a living organism to reproduce, or replicate. The nucleic acid inside the viral capsule carries the genetic information that is essential for replication of the virus. However, this is not enough for replication to take place. The

virus also requires the chemical building blocks and energy contained in living cells in order to reproduce. When a virus is not in a living cell it cannot replicate, though it may remain viable for some time. Scientists still do not agree that viruses are actually living things, since these entities cannot sustain life on their own.

LIFE IN A SINGLE-CELLED ORGANISM

There are many kinds of single-celled organisms that are not prokaryotes. Some of these single-celled eukaryotes look like slippers, vases, or balls. Some even have more than one nucleus. Many swim by waving a flagellum, a lashlike structure that looks like a thin arm or tail. Others use hairlike structures, which are called cilia. One kind has a mouth and a ring of moving "hairs" that bring in food. It also has a stalk that can stretch or coil up and pull the cell away from danger.

A well-known example of a single-celled eukaryote is the amoeba, a protozoan that lives in freshwater ponds. To the unaided eye it looks like a milky speck, but a microscope shows that the protozoan's "body" is composed largely of a jellylike substance called

cytoplasm that contains a nucleus and a number of specialized structures called organelles. The surface of the amoeba's cell is a clear, tough membrane that covers and protects the cytoplasm of the cell. The cell membrane is flexible and permits the amoeba to change shape as the cytoplasm flows within the cell. By doing so the amoeba can move to get food. It takes in a particle of food by surrounding it and enclosing it within a droplet called a vacuole. As it absorbs food, it grows. In due time it divides and each half takes its share of the cytoplasm. The two halves of the amoeba become two new amoebas.

Another example of life in a single eukaryotic cell may be seen in the tiny green algae known as *Protococcus*. Layers of these algae can form green scum on damp trees, rocks, and brick walls. Like the amoeba, each *Protococcus* cell contains cytoplasm and a nucleus as well as numerous organelles. The cell is covered with a membrane. The nucleus controls the life of the cell and in time divides for reproduction.

Inside the *Protococcus* cell is a chloroplast, a relatively large organelle filled with grains of chlorophyll. Using the energy of sunlight, these grains make food for the alga from water and carbon dioxide.

Organelles

The interior of a cell is organized into many specialized parts called organelles, each surrounded by a separate membrane. The nucleus is an organelle that contains the genetic information necessary for cell growth and reproduction. A cell contains only one nucleus, but it can contain multiple copies of other organelles. These include mitochondria, which produce the energy necessary for cell survival; lysosomes, which digest unwanted materials within the cell; and the endoplasmic reticulum and the Golgi apparatus, which make proteins and other important molecules and then transport them throughout the cell. In addition, plant cells and algae contain chloroplasts, which are responsible for photosynthesis.

Animal cells and plant cells contain membrane-bound organelles, including a distinct nucleus. In contrast, bacterial cells do not contain organelles. **Encyclopædia Britannica, Inc.**

Some Typical Cells

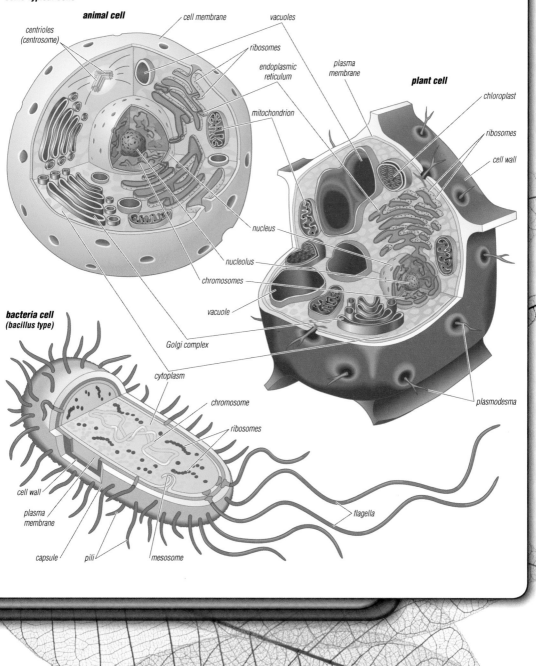

animal cell

centrioles (centrosome)

cell membrane

vacuoles

ribosomes

endoplasmic reticulum

plasma membrane

plant cell

chloroplast

ribosomes

cell wall

mitochondrion

nucleus

nucleolus

chromosomes

vacuole

Golgi complex

cytoplasm

plasmodesma

bacteria cell
(bacillus type)

chromosome

ribosomes

cell wall

plasma membrane

flagella

capsule

pili

mesosome

Since the alga can make food in this way, it does not have to move about like an amoeba. Therefore it can have a stiff, protecting wall, made of a transparent layer of cellulose. These two substances, chlorophyll and cellulose, are also found in plants.

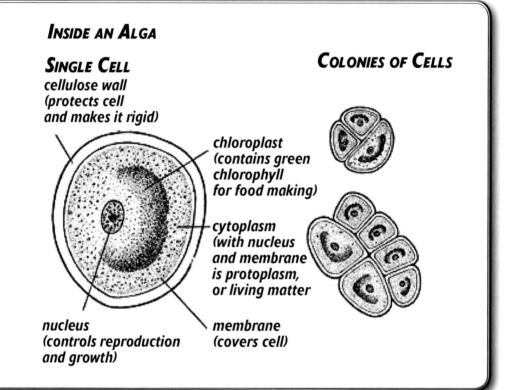

INSIDE AN ALGA

SINGLE CELL

cellulose wall
(protects cell
and makes it rigid)

chloroplast
(contains green
chlorophyll
for food making)

cytoplasm
(with nucleus
and membrane
is protoplasm,
or living matter

nucleus
(controls reproduction
and growth)

membrane
(covers cell)

COLONIES OF CELLS

The structure of the single-celled alga Protococcus *is similar in some ways to a plant cell. Algal cells, like those in plants, have a nucleus and a stiff cell wall made of cellulose. Floating in the cell's cytoplasm is a chloroplast, which contains chlorophyll. The chlorophyll uses energy from sunlight to make food from carbon dioxide and water. Colonies of these algae cells form green scum on ponds and moist rocks.* **Encyclopædia Britannica, Inc.**

MULTICELLULAR ORGANISMS

Plants and animals are much larger than viruses and microorganisms. They also are too big to be formed by a single cell. They therefore are made of many cells that live and work together.

Some of the simplest multicellular organisms are certain algae that live in ponds and streams. Each alga consists of a chain of cells that drifts about in the water. Most cells in the chain are alike, but the one at the bottom, called a holdfast, is different. It is long and tough. Its base holds to rocks or pieces of wood to keep the alga from floating away.

Sea lettuce, another type of multicellular algae, also has a holdfast. The rest of the plant contains boxlike cells arranged in two layers. These layers are covered and protected by two sheets of clear cellulose that is very tough.

Trees, weeds, and most other familiar land plants contain many more cells than sea lettuce and are much more complex. Their cells form organs such as roots, stems, leaves, and flowers. Millions of individual cells are needed to form these complex plants.

No animals consist simply of cells arranged in two flat layers like the sea lettuce. But the bodies of the pond-dwelling animals called hydras have just two layers of cells arranged in

a tube. The bottom of the tube is closed, but its top contains a mouth. Slender branches of the tube form tentacles that catch food and put it into the mouth.

Great numbers of cells of many kinds form the bodies of such creatures as insects, fish, and mammals. Similar cells that work together make up tissues. Tissues that work together form organs. A dog's heart, for example, is an organ composed of muscle tissue, nerve tissue, connective tissue, and covering tissue. Another kind of tissue, the blood, nourishes them. All these tissues work together when the dog's heart contracts.

THE ROLE OF HORMONES AND NERVE CELLS

The parts of a multicellular organism are controlled so that they work together. In plants, control is carried out by chemical substances called hormones. They go directly from cell to cell or are carried about in sap. When something touches a sensitive plant, for instance,

The brown hydra is a pond-dwelling creature composed of two layers of cells in a tubelike body. The two growths on either side of the pictured specimen are asexually reproduced buds , which will become new hydras. **Spike Walker/Stone/Getty Images**

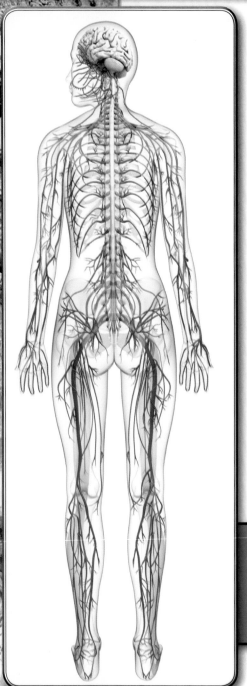

the touched cells produce a hormone that goes to countless other cells and makes them lose water and collapse. As cell after cell does this, leaves begin to droop. They will not spread out again until the effect of the hormones is lost.

In multicellular animals, hormones regulate growth, keep muscles in condition, and perform many similar tasks. Other controls are carried out by nerve cells via impulses to and from various parts of the body. These impulses can indicate that something has been seen, felt, or heard. They also make muscle cells contract or relax, so that animals can run, lie down, catch food, and do countless other things. Nerve cells may even deliver the impulses that stimulate hormone production.

The human nervous system controls muscle movement and sensory perception. Nerve cells connect to the spinal cord and brain via the central nervous system. **Dorling Kindersley/Getty Images**

MOLECULES AND ELEMENTS

When atoms, the basic units of chemical elements, combine into chemical compounds, they form molecules. Proteins and other types of molecules found in cells can be extremely complex. One such protein, called hemoglobin, carries oxygen in the blood and is what makes blood red. Hemoglobin contains atoms of six different elements — carbon, hydrogen, oxygen, nitrogen, sulfur, and iron.

The complexity is made possible by carbon, which may be called the framework element. Because of its structure, carbon can link different kinds of atoms in various proportions and arrangements. Carbon atoms also join with each other in long chains and other arrays to make some of the most complex compounds known to chemistry.

Three other commonly found elements, oxygen, hydrogen, and nitrogen, are also important in the structure and function of living things. In the human body, for example, these elements, together with carbon, make up about 96 percent of the body's weight. Oxygen and hydrogen are highly important in body processes that obtain and use energy

The elements oxygen and hydrogen help the human body absorb and process important nutrients found in food and water. Shutterstock.com

from food. Water, a compound of oxygen and hydrogen, plays a very important role in life processes. Large amounts of nitrogen are found in protein, or body-building compounds. Nitrogen also is found in wood and in the substance called chitin, which forms the shells of crustaceans, insects, jointed worms, and related creatures.

SPECIALIZATION

Single-celled organisms can have specialized parts, such as flagella or cilia, which are used in swimming as well as in setting up currents that bring food. The food is swallowed through a mouthlike structure and digested in droplets called vacuoles that circulate through the cellular cytoplasm. Special fibers that work like nerves control the cilia and flagella. Several unicellular organisms even possess specialized photoreceptors, sometimes called eyespots, that respond to light. All of these structures are said to be specialized because each one does its own part in the work of living.

In multicellular organisms, cells themselves are specialized. They become efficient in one process and are dependent upon other cells for other necessities of life. Multicellular

Adaptation

Specialization is carried from parts to entire living things. Cactus plants, for example, can live well only in dry regions, but cattails must grow in wet places. Herring swim near the surface of the sea, but the deep-sea angler fish lives on the bottom. Certain caterpillars eat only one kind of leaf.

This specialization of whole organisms is called adaptation. Every living thing is adapted to its surroundings — to the sea, freshwater, land, or even to living in or on other organisms. During the 3.5 billion years since living things evolved on Earth, organisms have become adapted to all sorts of conditions through the process known as evolution by natural selection. Today there are millions of different combinations between organisms and surroundings.

organisms also have tissues and organs that are still more specialized. Roots, leaves, flowers, eyes, and brains are examples of organs that do specialized work.

CHAPTER 3

NUTRITION AND ENERGY PRODUCTION

A ll living things require a constant supply of nutrients and energy to perform the tasks necessary for life. Depending on how they acquire these, organisms can be described as autotrophs or heterotrophs. Autotrophs are organisms that convert light or chemicals into nutrients and energy. They include algae and plants. Heterotrophs are organisms that acquire their energy by breaking down food. Human beings—like most other animals, fungi, protists, and bacteria—are heterotrophs.

HOW ALGAE AND PLANTS OBTAIN FOOD

All living things either make their food or get it ready-made. The single-celled alga *Protococcus* uses both methods. It uses photosynthesis to manufacture food from water and carbon dioxide. The process requires energy, which it obtains from sunlight. After several steps the food-making process results in a kind of sugar called glucose. This sugar is

An oak tree covered by a thin, green layer of Protococcus. *This form of algae gets nutrients through photosynthesis and by mixing glucose with other existing food sources. Shutterstock.com*

the fundamental nutrient required by all living cells for energy.

Protococcus may use glucose molecules almost as fast as it makes them. It also may turn them into starch or droplets of oil, which it stores for use when it cannot get sunlight. Finally, *Protococcus* may combine atoms from glucose with some ready-made food combinations in the dissolved minerals. In this way it builds up protoplasm and cellulose.

Plants also make glucose via photosynthesis. In doing so, however, they use many different cells, tissues, and organs, such as leaves, roots, and sap-carrying channels in the stem.

HOW ANIMALS OBTAIN FOOD

Although many animals are green, animals do not contain chlorophyll. Therefore they

A giraffe nibbling on treetop greenery gets nutrition from the glucose produced by the tree through photosynthesis. Shutterstock.com

cannot make food from carbon dioxide and water. This means that animals must get their food from other organisms, such as plants or other animals.

Like plants and algae, animals use food to produce different kinds of substances after they eat it. Animals use these substances for energy. They can turn sugary food into a starch called glycogen and store it in the liver, where it is ready for use when needed. When they eat more food than they need, they can store the extra food as fat.

SECURING ENERGY FROM FOOD

When plants make glucose from water and carbon dioxide, some atoms of oxygen are released from the combined materials. More oxygen is lost when glucose is converted into common sugar, starch, fat, or other food substances. As oxygen is removed, energy is stored in the made-over molecules.

The stored energy can later be obtained by cells through what is essentially a reverse process called oxidation. In a complex series of steps, oxygen is combined with food molecules, which change into simpler substances and give up energy. If complete oxidation takes place, the food becomes water and

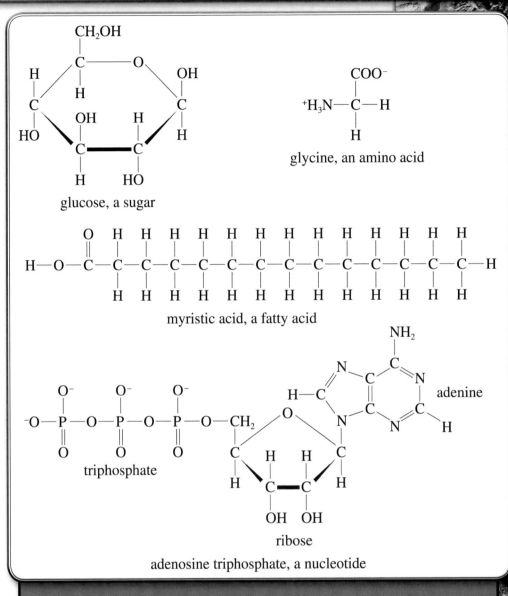

Examples of members of the four families of small organic molecules: sugars (e.g., glucose), amino acids (e.g., glycine), fatty acids (e.g., myristic acid), and nucleotides (e.g., adenosine triphosphate, or ATP). Encyclopædia Britannica, Inc.

carbon dioxide again and gives up all its stored energy. Part of this energy is lost, but most of it remains available to the cell to carry out the functions of living.

Some organisms, especially micro-organisms, can live in environments with little to no oxygen. These organisms also secure energy through chemical processes that change foods into simpler compounds. In one such process, called alcoholic fermentation, food gives up stored energy and changes into ethanol (a form of alcohol) and carbon dioxide. Alcoholic fermentation by yeast organisms in bread dough, for example, changes sugar into alcohol and carbon dioxide. The carbon dioxide is what makes the dough rise, and the alcohol evaporates as the bread is baked.

CARRYING FOOD, OXYGEN, AND WASTE PRODUCTS

Single-celled organisms such as *Protococcus* get food-making substances and energy through their cell wall. In multicellular plants each cell also exchanges substances through its wall. To provide what every cell needs and to carry off wastes the plant uses a liquid called sap, which travels through specialized cells in the plant.

ATP—THE POWER MOLECULE

Adenosine triphosphate, or ATP for short, is an energy-carrying molecule found in the cells of all living things. ATP captures chemical energy obtained from the breakdown of food molecules and releases it to fuel other cellular processes.

Cells require chemical energy for three general types of tasks: to drive metabolic reactions that would not occur automatically; to transport needed substances across membranes; and to do mechanical work, such as moving muscles. ATP is not a storage molecule for chemical energy; that is the job of carbohydrates and fats. But when energy is needed by the cell, it is converted from storage molecules into ATP. ATP then serves as a shuttle, delivering energy to places within the cell where energy-consuming activities are taking place. Although cells continuously break down ATP to obtain energy, ATP is also constantly being produced through the processes of cellular respiration.

A drop of sap drips from a tree. Sap transports necessary nutrients to the tree's many cells and helps rid plant life of waste products. free_spirit@photos/Flickr/Getty Images

The larger multicellular animals provide for the needs of their cells with circulating liquids called blood and lymph. Blood carries oxygen and nutrients from digested food to the body's cells, and it carries away the carbon dioxide and water produced as wastes by cellular processes. Lymph is a fluid that circulates through its own system in the body, playing an important role in the immune system as well as helping the blood dispose of wastes from tissues.

CHAPTER 4

EVOLUTION AND THE HISTORY OF LIFE ON EARTH

The evidence is overwhelming that all life on Earth has evolved from common ancestors in an unbroken chain since its origin. The theory of evolution, put forth in the 19th century by English naturalist Charles Darwin, explains how the diverse species of living things have descended from those common ancestors. The theory revolutionized the study of living things and remains central to the foundations of modern biology.

HERITABILITY OF TRAITS

Darwin's theory of evolution is summarized by the following facts. All life tends to increase. More organisms are conceived, born, hatched, germinated from seed, sprouted from spores, or produced by cell division than can possibly survive. Each organism varies, however little, in some way

Major Evolutionary Events, 650 million years ago to the present

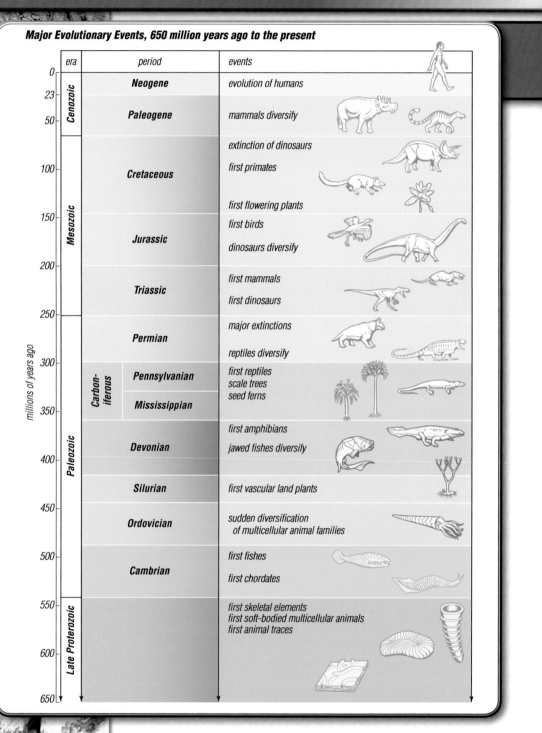

millions of years ago	era	period		events
0	Cenozoic	Neogene		evolution of humans
23				
50		Paleogene		mammals diversify
100	Mesozoic	Cretaceous		extinction of dinosaurs first primates first flowering plants
150		Jurassic		first birds dinosaurs diversify
200		Triassic		first mammals first dinosaurs
250	Paleozoic	Permian		major extinctions reptiles diversify
300		Carboniferous	Pennsylvanian	first reptiles scale trees seed ferns
350			Mississippian	
400		Devonian		first amphibians jawed fishes diversify
		Silurian		first vascular land plants
450		Ordovician		sudden diversification of multicellular animal families
500		Cambrian		first fishes first chordates
550	Late Proterozoic			first skeletal elements first soft-bodied multicellular animals first animal traces
600				
650				

from its relatives. In any given environment at any given time, the organisms with traits best suited to that environment will tend to leave more offspring than the others. Offspring resemble their ancestors. Variant organisms will leave offspring like themselves. Therefore, organisms will diverge, or separate, from their ancestors with time.

The term natural selection is shorthand for saying that all organisms do not survive to leave offspring with the same probability. Those alive today have been selected relative to similar ones that never survived or reproduced. All organisms on Earth today are equally evolved because all share the same ancient original ancestors who faced innumerable threats to their survival. All have persisted since the early part of the Archean eon, some 3.5 billion years ago.

CONVERGENT EVOLUTION

The environment of Earth is varied. Mountains, oceans, and deserts suffer

Adaptive radiation in Galapagos finches

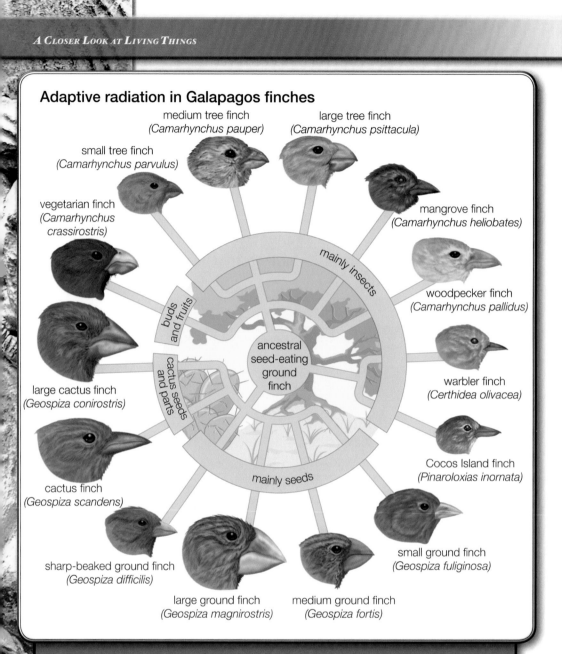

Fourteen species of Galapagos finches that evolved from a common ancestor. The different shapes of their bills, suited to different diets and habitats, illustrate the evolutionary process called adaptive radiation. Encyclopædia Britannica, Inc.

extremes of temperature, humidity, and water availability. All ecosystems contain habitats that appear unfavorable to life; oceanic oozes lacking oxygen, for example, or boiling springs. For each environmental condition, however, there is a corresponding ecological niche—that is, a place for a specially adapted organism to live and thrive. The variety of ecological niches populated on Earth is quite remarkable. Even wet

A young spinner dolphin swims with its mother in the Red Sea. Their streamlined shape mimicks that of other sea animals in an example of convergent evolution. Shutterstock.com

A red "eye" spot, as seen near the upper left end of this Euglena spirogyra *specimen, is an evolutionary trait that has developed independently in protists and animals alike.* **Wim van Egmond/Visuals Unlimited/ Getty Images**

cracks in granite are alive with "rock eating" bacteria.

As life has evolved over billions of years, different organisms have filled particular ecological niches independently several times. For example, the same streamlined shape for high-speed motion in seawater evolved independently at least four times: in prehistoric reptiles; in tuna, which are fish; and in dolphins and seals, which are mammals.

LIFE ON OTHER PLANETS?

No one knows if extraterrestrial life, or life that originated beyond Earth, exists or ever existed. The branch of biology concerned with extra-terrestrial life, from microscopic organisms to intelligent beings, is called exobiology or astro-biology. Scientists in this field consider the conditions necessary for life, how it evolves, how to detect alien life-forms, and the environments in which they might live, whether in our own solar system or on any of the numerous planets orbiting other stars.

The precise requirements for life are not known. All living things on Earth (which are all related) are structurally based on carbon and need water as a medium for chemical reactions. Hydrogen, nitrogen, phosphorous, sulfur, oxy-gen, and other elements are also essential. However, if alien life-forms exist, they might be fundamentally different from any living thing on Earth. Such life-forms might be dif-ficult to detect or even recognize as life. At a basic level, living things must be made of atoms that bond to form a variety of molecules at the temperatures in their environment. They also probably require a liquid (water, or per-haps ammonia, hydrogen cyanide, or liquid hydrocarbons) to act as a solvent for chemical reactions. The environment, then, would have liquid at or near the surface. It would also need sunlight or another energy source, protection from ultraviolet radiation, and probably an atmosphere.

Exploration of the solar system, of course, has been an important part of the search for extraterrestrial life. Unmanned probes have visited every planet in the solar system, plus many moons, asteroids, and comets. Places in the solar system that seem most likely to have harbored life—most likely microbes—include Mars, Jupiter's moon Europa, and Saturn's moon Enceladus. All three have, or once had, liquid water at or near the surface. Saturn's moon Titan, which appears to have lakes of liquid methane, is also of great interest. With its geologic activity and dense, nitrogen-rich atmosphere with a haze of organic compounds, Titan in several ways resembles primordial Earth.

This phenomenon is called convergent evolution. It means that when there is one most efficient solution to a given ecological problem, different kinds of organisms will often evolve similar, nearly identical solutions. In the case of the streamlined form of sea animals, convergent evolution resulted from the fact that there is only a narrow range of solutions to the problem of high-speed motion by large animals in the sea.

Another example of convergent evolution is the eye. A light receptor that makes an image, the eye has evolved independently more than two dozen times, not only in animals but in some of the lower organisms called protists. Apparently eyelike structures best solve the problem of visual recording.

SPONTANEOUS GENERATION

Before the 16th century it was commonly believed that organisms such as flies and worms arose from mud or other nonliving substances. This idea is known as spontaneous generation. According to the theory, pieces of cheese and bread wrapped in rags and left in a dark corner were thought to produce mice, because after several weeks mice appeared in the rags. Many people believed in spontaneous generation because it explained such occurrences as maggots swarming on decaying meat.

By the 18th century it had become obvious that plants and animals could not be produced by nonliving material. The origin of microorganisms such as yeast and bacteria, however, was not fully determined

Experiments disproving spontaneous generation

Francesco Redi 1668 experiment

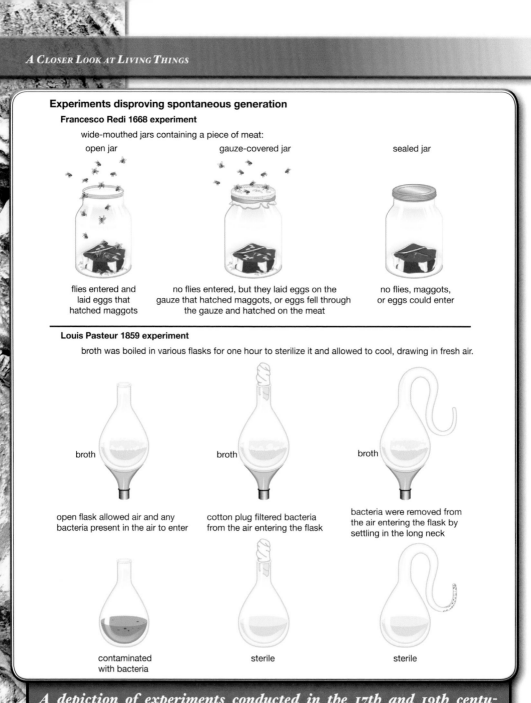

wide-mouthed jars containing a piece of meat:

open jar   gauze-covered jar   sealed jar

flies entered and laid eggs that hatched maggots

no flies entered, but they laid eggs on the gauze that hatched maggots, or eggs fell through the gauze and hatched on the meat

no flies, maggots, or eggs could enter

Louis Pasteur 1859 experiment

broth was boiled in various flasks for one hour to sterilize it and allowed to cool, drawing in fresh air.

broth   broth   broth

open flask allowed air and any bacteria present in the air to enter

cotton plug filtered bacteria from the air entering the flask

bacteria were removed from the air entering the flask by settling in the long neck

contaminated with bacteria   sterile   sterile

A depiction of experiments conducted in the 17th and 19th centuries designed to disprove the concept of spontaneous generation. **Encyclopædia Britannica, Inc.**

until French chemist Louis Pasteur proved in the 19th century that microorganisms reproduce, that all organisms come from preexisting organisms, and that all cells come from preexisting cells.

BIOPOIESIS

Although the doctrine of spontaneous generation was rejected in the 19th century, a similar idea has been put forth to explain the origin of life on Earth. Biopoiesis is a process by which living organisms are thought to develop from nonliving matter. According to the biopoiesis theory, conditions were such that, at one time in Earth's history, life was created from nonliving material, probably in the sea, which contained the necessary chemicals. During this process, molecules slowly grouped, then regrouped, forming ever more efficient means for energy transformation and becoming capable of reproduction.

Some scientists think that under present conditions new forms of life are not likely to be created from nonliving matter. Others feel that life is continuously being created but that the new forms are not so well adapted to the environment as existing ones and are thus unable to compete successfully.

THE GEOLOGIC RECORD

Past time on Earth is divided into four immense periods of time called eons. These are the Hadean (4.6 to 4 billion years ago), the Archean (4 to 2.5 billion years ago), the Proterozoic (2.5 billion to 542 million years ago), and the Phanerozoic (542 million years ago to the present).

Evidence of the earliest primitive life-forms appears in rocks dating from about 3.5 billion years ago, during the Archean eon. The microorganisms preserved in these fossils are bacteria, including the type known as cyanobacteria. Some of these simple prokaryotes began carrying out photosynthesis, making their own food and releasing oxygen into the atmosphere. During the Proterozoic eon, the level of oxygen in the atmosphere reached levels that enabled more complex organisms to evolve.

The earliest fossils are all of aquatic organisms. Cyanobacteria that lived on land did not appear until about 2 billion years ago. By the dawn of the Phanerozoic eon, however, life had established itself firmly both on land and in the waters of the world. For example, the major groups of marine animals such as mollusks (snails, clams, squid) and arthropods

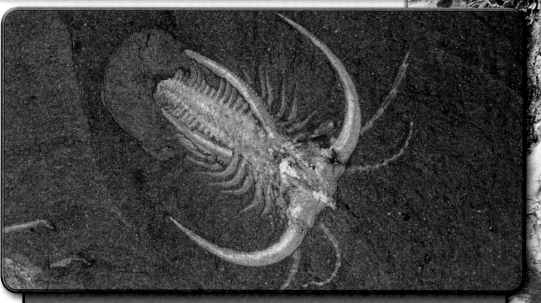

Fossils, such as that of this ancient anthropod known as a **Marrella,** *confirm the existence of life on Earth hundreds of millions of years ago.* O. Louis Mazzatenta/National Geographic Image Collection/ Getty Images

(crabs, lobsters) appeared for the first time about 542 million years ago at the start of the Cambrian period of the Phanerozoic eon. Vascular plants began to form colonies along coastal lowlands during the Silurian period, 444 to 416 million years ago.

Over time, living things developed more and more ways of adapting to more and more environments. Some species became extinct, but others persisted and changed. Eventually the process of evolution produced the full range of living things known today.

CHAPTER 5

THE CLASSIFICATION OF LIVING THINGS

Some scientists estimate that there are roughly 14 million species on Earth, though only approximately 1.9 million have been identified. For centuries scientists divided living things into two kingdoms—plants and animals. Most organisms classified in the plant kingdom had chlorophyll and cellulose. The animal kingdom consisted of species that lacked chlorophyll or cellulose. This classification system was formalized in the 18th century by the biologist Carolus Linnaeus. The system of Linnaeus was based on similarities in body structure, and it was completed more than a hundred years before the work of Charles Darwin, whose theory of evolution showed that the similarities and differences of organisms could be viewed as a product of evolution by natural selection.

As biologists in the 20th century learned more about microorganisms and fungi, they recognized the need for a different classification system that would draw on the evolutionary relationships among organisms. A five-kingdom system began to be adopted

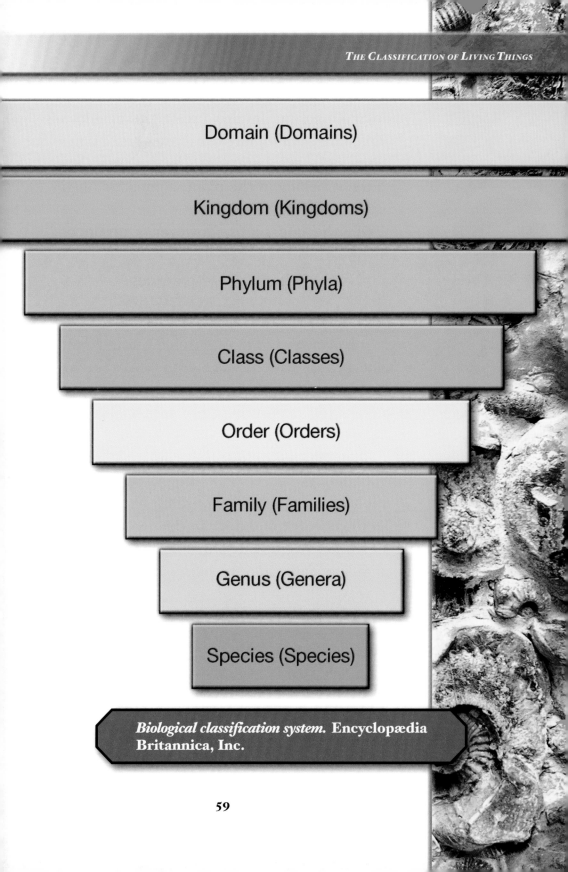

Domain (Domains)

Kingdom (Kingdoms)

Phylum (Phyla)

Class (Classes)

Order (Orders)

Family (Families)

Genus (Genera)

Species (Species)

Biological classification system. Encyclopædia Britannica, Inc.

in the 1970s that separated fungi into their own kingdom. It also created a kingdom called Monera for all prokaryotes and a kingdom called Protista for all eukaryotes that did not belong in the plant, animal, or fungi kingdoms.

In the late 1970s, however, a group of scientists determined the existence of a previously unknown form of life. Using molecular technology to examine the evolutionary relationship among several groups of prokaryotes, the researchers noted that one group had distinct differences in its genetic code that set it apart from other prokaryotes. This finding eventually led to a significant modification in the classification of living things because these organisms, now called archaea, became recognized by most biologists as one of three distinct branches of life that formed early in the development of life on Earth. The three branches, called domains, are the Archaea, Bacteria, and Eukarya.

BACTERIA

Bacteria are single-celled prokaryotes (organisms with no distinct nuclei or organelles). Virtually all bacteria have a rigid cell wall,

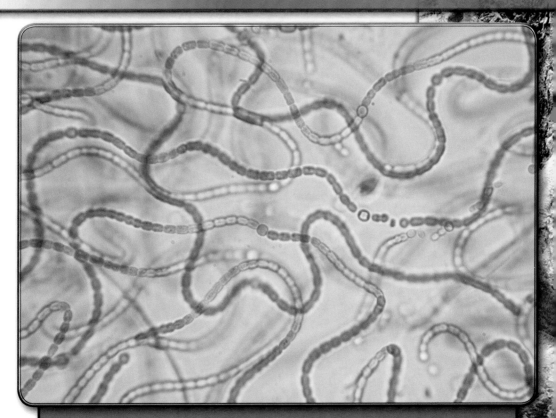

*A **microscopic** view of* Nostoc *cyanobacteria arranged in beadlike chains.* **Dr. James Richardson/Visuals Unlimited/Getty Images**

which contains a substance called peptidogly-can. Typical shapes of bacteria cells include spheres, rods, and spirals. Some bacteria have flagella that they use to propel themselves. Based on genetic studies experts believe there may be approximately 1 million species of bacteria, of which only roughly 4,000 have been identified.

As a group, bacteria are highly diverse. Some bacteria are aerobic and others are anaerobic. Some, such as purple bacteria and cyanobacteria, contain chlorophyll and therefore can make their own food. Purple bacteria swim by means of flagella. Although they are photosynthetic, the greenish particles they contain are a different form of chlorophyll than that found in other photosynthetic organisms. Cyanobacteria have no flagella and often live together in chains or clumps covered by a jellylike substance. They contain true chlorophyll and thus are autotrophic. However, under certain conditions they may also take in food from other sources. Most bacteria are heterotrophic, including an important group of bacteria that decompose the matter from dead organisms. Other important groups of bacteria include disease-causing bacteria and bacteria that convert nitrogen in the air into compounds that plants can use.

ARCHAEA

Archaea, like bacteria, are single-celled prokaryotes, and their external appearance is similar to that of bacteria. Nevertheless,

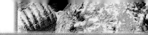

Archaea are found in a diverse range of extreme environments, including the salt deposits on the shores of the Dead Sea. Z. Radovan, Jerusalem

they differ from bacteria genetically and in terms of structural components and biochemistry. For example, the cell wall of archaea does not contain peptidoglycan and the way archaea process DNA is more complex. Although abundant numbers of archaea live in a great variety of habitats,

63

including in the oceans and in soil, a notable characteristic of certain species is that they can thrive in environments that are deadly to other kinds of organisms.

Many archaea inhabit the deep vents on the ocean floor or hot springs, where temperatures are well over 200 °F (93 °C). *Pyrococcus woesei* is a notable example. It grows at temperatures above 212 °F (100 °C). Other such extremophile species of archaea live in pools of highly acidic or salty water. Archaea known as methanogens live in environments such as swamp mud or in the rumens of cows, where there is no oxygen. They take in carbon dioxide and hydrogen from their environment and produce methane gas as a by-product of their metabolism.

In a sense, these habitats resemble some of the early conditions on Earth, such as boiling hot water springs and an atmosphere devoid of oxygen. The ability of archaea to thrive in such extreme conditions suggests that they had become adapted to them long ago, and the pattern of the genetic code of archaea has suggested that these organisms were probably among the earliest forms of life on Earth. In other comparisons with bacteria, some archaea, like certain bacteria, are able to make nitrogen in the atmosphere available to plants. Unlike bacteria, no species of archaea has been found that uses chlorophyll for photosynthesis and no archaea that cause disease in humans has been identified.

Archaea are difficult to identify and study because most cannot be grown in a laboratory culture. Advances in DNA techniques, however, make it possible to analyze directly material from the environment to identify the DNA and RNA of the archaea and other microorganisms inhabiting the sample.

EUKARYA

The domain Eukarya encompasses all organisms other than bacteria and archaea. It includes both single-celled protists such as algae and protozoa and multicellular organisms such as fungi, plants, and animals.

PROTISTS

Protists are a very diverse group of mostly single-celled organisms that are eukaryotes — that is, they have a true nucleus and organelles — and are not considered to belong

to the animal, plant, or fungi kingdoms. They may live as solitary individuals or in groups called colonies, and they may be autotrophic or heterotrophic.

Under the five-kingdom classification protists made up the kingdom Protista, and under the three-domain system most biologists continued to use that classification. Advances in comparing the genetic information from many kinds of protists indicated,

The bite of the tsetse fly is responsible for infecting people with the protist Trypanosoma brucei, *which is responsible for the onset of an often deadly disease called African sleeping sickness.* **John Cooke/ Oxford Scientific/Getty Images**

however, that new kingdoms might be needed for their classification and researchers sought to characterize them. It is estimated that there are some 600,000 species of protists on Earth, but only a fraction of these—roughly 80,000—have been described.

Many protists live in the oceans or in freshwater. The protists are commonly divided into the animal-like protozoa, most of which are heterotrophic; the plantlike algae, which are autotrophic; and the fungus-like slime molds and water molds, which feed on decaying matter. Some protozoa have flagella or cilia to help propel them through their environment. This helps them to capture food and evade predators. Protozoa such as the euglenoids have chlorophyll and can make glucose via photosynthesis, though they may also capture food from outside sources under certain conditions. Algae also are autotrophic and manufacture food via photosynthesis.

A number of protists cause important diseases. The flagellate protist *Trypanosoma brucei* causes the disease African sleeping sickness in humans, while a particular species of amoeba is responsible for a form of dysentery.

A mushroom grows on a tree trunk. Mushrooms and other fungi depend on living organisms or dead organic matter for food. Shutterstock.com

FUNGI

The fungi kingdom contains a widely diverse group of organisms, ranging from yeasts to molds and mildews to mushrooms and toadstools. A fungus is categorized as a heterotrophic eukaryotic organism with cell walls. In addition, all fungi are multicellular. The presence of cell walls in these organisms inspired biologists to classify them for many years with the plants. However, fungi possess many traits not found in plants. Fungi lack chlorophyll and chloroplasts; they cannot synthesize their own food but rather must depend on other organisms for nourishment.

Many fungi do this via symbiotic relationships with other organisms. Like animals, fungi must digest their food before absorbing it, but unlike animals, fungi digest their food outside of their bodies. To do this, fungi secrete enzymes into their immediate surroundings; these enzymes degrade, or break down, food into small molecules that are then absorbed by the fungi. According to scientific estimates, there are roughly 1.5 million species of fungi on Earth, though only 80,000 are known.

Symbiosis

Close living arrangements between two different species is called symbiosis. The word comes from the Greek word meaning "state of living together." Usually the two organisms are in close physical contact, with one living on or in the other. In some cases, however, the relationship is less intimate.

Symbiosis is classified into mutualism (once called symbiosis), commensalism, and parasitism. In mutualism both partners benefit from the relationship. Commensalism describes a relationship in which one member benefits while the other is neither helped nor harmed. In parasitism one member of the relationship benefits while the other is harmed.

In a classic symbiotic relationship, clownfish live unharmed among the stinging tentacles of sea anemones, where they are protected from predators. **Shutterstock.com**

PLANTS

The plants are multicellular eukaryotic organisms and are classified in the kingdom Plantae. Members of the plant kingdom range from simple green vines and moss to enormous complex trees such as redwoods. Biologists believe there are approximately 300,000 species of plants. Of these, an estimated 10 percent have not been identified,

Snakeskin liverwort growing in Great Smoky Mountains National Park, Tennessee. Liverworts are one of a handful of terrestrial plants that are nonvascular. **Altrendo/Getty Images**

and experts believe most of these exist in rain forests.

Virtually all plants contain chlorophyll and are autotrophs. Some plants are vascular—that is, they have specialized tissues that carry water and nutrients to all parts of the plant. Vascular plants include the flowering plants, the trees, and most familiar terrestrial plants. Other plants are nonvascular; they lack roots, stems, and leaves and are usually aquatic. Some terrestrial plants, including mosses and liverworts, also are nonvascular. Terrestrial nonvascular plants are usually small. Their lack of a vascular system limits the amounts of nutrients that can be transported to all of their cells.

A few species of plants such as dodder and Indian pipe are nonphotosynthetic parasites. A few others such as the Venus's-flytrap are photosynthetic but carnivorous—they trap insects as a source of nitrogen and minerals.

ANIMALS

The organisms classified in the kingdom Animalia are multicellular eukaryotes. Because their cells lack chlorophyll, all animals are heterotrophs. They have different types of tissues in their bodies and usually can move freely. Animals are sometimes called metazoans, which thus distinguishes them from the protozoans, which are single-celled.

Animals can be divided into two main groups: invertebrates and vertebrates. The invertebrates—such as insects, sea stars (starfish), and worms—lack a backbone. The body tissues of many invertebrates are supported by some type of outer structure, called an exoskeleton. Vertebrates have a backbone. Animals categorized as vertebrates include fish; amphibians, such as frogs and salamanders; reptiles, such as snakes and lizards; birds; and mammals such as dogs, cows, horses, monkeys, and humans.

A cicada sloughs off its exoskeleton. Because invertebrates such as the cicada lack a backbone, they are supported, and their tissue protected, by the hard covering of an exoskeleton. **Richard Ellis/ Getty Images**

The animal kingdom is by far the largest kingdom of eukaryotes. Experts believe that there are more than 10 million species of animals living today; of these, only about 1.3 million species have been identified. The largest group within the animal kingdom is the insects. Roughly 8 million species of insects may exist, but only about 1 million have been identified or described. The best known of the animal groups are birds and mammals, of which roughly 10,000 and 4,500 species have been identified, respectively.

The diversity of the living world is staggering. Nearly 2 million species of organisms have been named and described, and many millions more remain to be discovered. What is impressive is not just the numbers but also the incredible variety of sizes, shapes, and ways of life. Living things range from lowly bacteria, measuring less than a thousandth of a millimeter in diameter, to stately sequoias, rising 300 feet (100 meters) above the ground and weighing thousands of tons; from bacteria living in hot springs at temperatures near the boiling point of water to fungi and algae thriving on the ice masses of Antarctica; and from giant tube worms living near deep vents on the dark ocean floor to spiders and larkspur plants existing on the slopes of Mount Everest more than 19,700 feet (6,000 meters) above sea level. With so much diversity on display—and with so much of the living world still undiscovered—the identification and classification of living things will remain a dynamic and essential pursuit among biologists, and an area of acute interest of curious minds everywhere.

aerobic Living, active, or occurring only in the presence of oxygen.

archaea Any of a group of single-celled prokaryotic organisms that look like bacteria but are structurally different.

autotroph An organism that makes it own food by harnessing sunlight through photosynthesis; compare to heterotrophs, which must eat other organisms for food.

bacteria Any of a group of single-celled microorganisms that live in soil, water, organic matter, or the bodies of plants and animals.

cellulose A complex carbohydrate that is the main component of plant cell walls.

chloroplast A structure within a green plant cell in which photosynthesis occurs.

cilia Tiny hairlike structures that help single-celled organisms move.

eukaryote Any organism composed of one or more cells, each of which contains a clearly defined nucleus enclosed by a membrane, along with organelles.

extremophile An organism that lives under extreme environmental conditions such as in a hot spring or ice cap.

flagellum A long whiplike structure, the motion of which helps some microscopic organisms move.

fungi Multicellular organisms that are like plants but lack chlorophyll, and therefore depend on other organisms to gain nutrients.

heterotroph An organism that breaks down an existing food source to receive nutrients; compare to autotrophs, which use sunlight and chemicals to create food.

meristem Region of cells capable of division and growth in plants.

metazoa A scientific term for animals, which have bodies composed of multiple cells forming tissues and organs; as opposed to single-celled protazoa.

methanogen Any of various anaerobic microorganisms that produce methane as a result of metabolizing, or processing, carbon dioxide and hydrogen.

photosynthesis The process by which green plants transform light energy into chemical energy.

prokaryote A typically single-celled microorganism that lacks a distinct nucleus and membrane-bound organelles.

protist Any of a large group of mostly single-celled organisms that resemble plants or animals but are classified as neither; they include the protozoa, algae, and some lower fungi.

protozoan Any of a group of single-celled organisms that have varied structure and physiology and often complicated life cycles.

stoma A microscopic opening or pore in the top layer of a leaf or young stem.

symbiosis A close living arrangement between two organisms that benefits either one or both of the two.

vascular Of or relating to tissues through which a life-giving, nutrient-rich fluid, such as blood (animals) or water (plants), flows through an organism's body.

American Institute of Biological Sciences
1900 Campus Commons Drive
Suite 200
Reston, VA 20191
(703) 674-2500
Web site: http://www.aibs.org
The American Institute of Biological
    Sciences offers a number of programs
    and resources that include publications,
    biological research, and advisory services
    to U.S. government agencies.

American Society for Microbiology
1752 N Street NW
Washington, DC 20036-2904
(202) 737-3600
Web site: http://www.asm.org
The American Society for Microbiology
    advances the study of microorganisms
    through fellowships, online publications,
    conferences, and workshops.

Canadian Museum of Nature
PO Box 3443, Station D
Ottawa, ON K1P 6P4
Canada
(613) 566-4700
Web site: http://nature.ca/en/home

The Canadian Museum of Nature is the
country's national natural history
museum, featuring exhibits and activities
concerning the living Earth.

Environment Canada
351 St. Joseph Boulevard
Place Vincent Massey
Gatineau, QC K1A 0H3
Canada
(819) 997-2800
Web site: http://www.ec.gc.ca
Environment Canada is a national organi-
zation that works to protect Canada's
natural resources. As such, it has access
to extensive research and databases concerning the country's biodiversity and
burgeoning new species.

The Linnaean Society of New York
PO Box 4121
New York, NY 10163-4121
Web site: http://linnaeannewyork.org
Members of the Linnaean Society of New
York share an active interest in observ-
ing and learning about the natural
environment of New York state and its
inhabitants. The society publishes a

newsletter, holds meetings, and sponsors field trips, with a special emphasis on ornithology.

National Museum of Natural History
PO Box 37012, Smithsonian Institution
Washington, DC 20013-7012
Web site: http://www.mnh.si.edu
With more than 126 million specimens and artifacts in its collections, the National Museum of Natural History inspires public interest in all aspects of the natural world and offers numerous resources for those wishing to explore the planet's biodiversity.

WEB SITES

Due to the changing nature of Internet links, Rosen Educational Services has developed an online list of Web sites related to the subject of this book. This site is updated regularly. Please use this link to access the list:

http://www.rosenlinks.com/biol/lvth

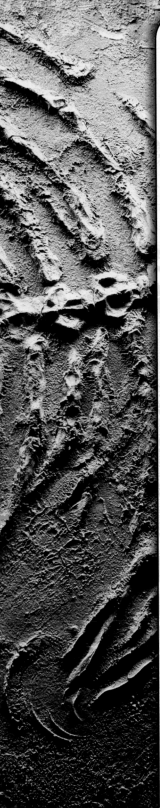

BIBLIOGRAPHY

Ackroyd, Peter. *The Beginning* (DK, 2004).

Bright, Michael. *Extinctions of Living Things* (Heinemann, 2009).

Diversity of Living Things (McDougal Littell, 2007).

Light, Douglas. *Cells, Tissues, and Skin* (Chelsea House, 2009).

Maczulak, Anne. *Biodiversity: Conserving Endangered Species* (Facts on File, 2010).

Miller, D.A. *Biodiversity* (Greenhaven, 2008).

Silverstein, Alvin, et al. *Growth and Development* (Twenty-First Century Books, 2008).

Silverstein, Alvin, et al. *Symbiosis*, rev. ed. (Twenty-First Century Books, 2008).

Snedden, Robert. *The Diversity of Life: From Single Cells to Multicellular Organisms*, rev ed. (Heinemann, 2008).

Spicer, John. *Biodiversity: A Beginner's Guide* (Oneworld, 2006).

Vogt, Gregory. *The Biosphere: Realm of Life* (Twenty-First Century Books, 2007).

H

habitats, 10, 24, 25, 29,
36, 47–49, 56–57,
63–64, 67
Hadean eon, 56
healing, 18–19
hemoglobin, 33
heterotrophs, 23, 37, 62,
66, 67, 69, 72–74
"higher" organisms, 20
holdfasts, 29
hormones, 31–32
humans, 13, 19, 33, 37, 65,
67, 74
hydrogen, 11, 12, 33, 35,
51, 64

I

immune systems, 44
injuries, 18–19
insects, 15, 31, 35, 72, 73, 74
invertebrates, 73
iron, 33

L

leaves, 15, 29, 32, 36, 39
light, 13, 25, 35, 37, 51, 53
Linnaeus, Carolus, 58
"lower" organisms, 20
lungs, 13
lymph, 44
lysosomes, 26

M

mammals, 13, 15, 20, 31, 33,
37, 50, 65, 67, 73, 74
Mars, 52
metabolic reactions, 43
metazoans, 73
methane, 52, 64
methanogens, 64
mitochondria, 26
molds, 67
molecular technology, 60
molecules, 12, 26, 33–35,
43, 51
Monera, 60
movement, 12, 24, 25, 28,
35, 61, 62, 67, 7e
multicellular organisms,
13, 29–32, 35–36,
42, 44, 65, 69,
71–74
muscles, 31, 32, 43
mutualism, 69, 70

N

natural selection, 12, 36,
45–47, 58
nerve cells, 31–32
nitrate, 15
nitrogen, 15, 33, 35, 51, 52,
62, 65
nuclei, 21, 24, 25, 26,
60, 65
nucleic acid, 12, 23